KESTNER
and
SIMON & HALBIG DOLLS
1804 - 1930

by Patricia R. Smith

Edited by: *Tyral Jane Weiss*
Photo's By: *Dwight F. Smith*

Copyright: Patricia Smith - Bill Schroeder 1976
ISBN - 0-89145-022-X

D1097223

Additional Copies of this book may be ordered at $7.95 Postpaid from:

COLLECTOR BOOKS
P.O. Box 3009
Paducah, Kentucky 42001

CONTENTS

OTHER BOOKS BY AUTHOR

Modern Collector's Dolls, Series 1 . . . . $17.95
Modern Collector's Dolls, Series 11 . . . . 17.95
Modern Collector's Dolls, Series 111 . . . . 17.95
Antique Collector's Dolls, Series 1 . . . . 17.95
Armand Marseille Dolls 7.95

Postpaid

cb

ORDER FROM:
COLLECTOR BOOKS
P.O. Box 3009
Paducah, Kentucky 42001

The main and of utmost importance to any doll is the head. The quality of the bisque and that it is not damaged in any way, is the determining factor for which prices should be based. That means no hairline cracks, cracked or broken shoulder plates, eye chips, any mends or repairs, etc. and that the quality of the bisque is very good to excellent.

The most desirable dolls are completely perfect, original, in original boxes and unplayed with. But prices based on this assumption are unrealistic because the ratio is an overwhelming 6,000 to 1. That leaves 5,999 dolls showing varying degrees of use. . .so the prices in this book are based on the quality of the head alone. These prices are for excellent quality bisque in perfect condition and with no defects.

Body rubs, a missing finger, a crack in the kid, a minor repair to the foot, etc. (These are all minor, not major damages), play no part in the prices in this book and I have not gone into great detail on bodies because who can say what is original or not. After all, many, many heads and bodies were replaced when the dolls were toys and for various reasons, bisque heads did break and were replaced, parts of bodies were destroyed and replaced.

The prices for this book were not made up. They cover a four year study of Kestner and Simon & Halbig dolls as they have been sold through dealers in the United States.

If a doll is more that I have based prices on. . .that is, all original, in an original box and unplayed with. . .you can add 30% over and above these prices!!

Collectors set their own prices by what they are willing to pay for any certain dolls.

I have used a scale method of pricing to allow for the quality of the bisque.

A	$50.00
B	100.00
C	150.00
D	200.00
E	250.00
F	300.00
G	350.00
H	400.00
I	450.00
J	500.00
K	600.00
L	700.00
M	800.00
N	900.00
O	1,000.00
P	1,050.00
Q	1,100.00
R	1,200.00
S	1,300.00
T	1,450.00
U	1,700.00
V	1,900.00
W	2,200.00
X	2,400.00
Y	2,700.00
Z	3,000.00

THE J.D. KESTNER STORY

The following is from the "Playthings" magazine of April 1906 on the Kestner Factory.

One of the largest factories turning out a leading and fast selling line of modern dolls was established early in the last century at Waltershausen. Here a young man, named John Daniel Kestner in a small way began manufacturing memorandum-slates from paper pulp, gradually increasing his lines until he was turning out toys such as wood pop-guns, wood limb dolls, etc.

The manufacturer of dolls improved step by step. First wood limb dolls with wood or paper pulp heads, then the wood bodies were replaced with paper pulp ones. About 1845 the first dolls wearing chemise, shoes, stockings, and hood were placed on the market. Next on a very small scale muslin and kid dolls were turned out.

About fifteen years later a marked advance was made when porcelain heads and limbs were introduced, also paper pulp with a wax covering. At this time, too, the Papa-Mama dolls were introduced, and Kestner invented the sleeping doll with movable eyes.

Human hair was used chiefly on the heads but this was substituted by so-call mohair which is really the hair of the Angora goat. Now, in addition to the ordinary dolls with muslin or kid bodies, fine jointed kid, and papier-mache jointed dolls, enamel finished with loose ball joints are made in large quantities. The heads are porcelain, or indestructible, of paper pulp or celluloid.

Since about 1815, almost one hundred years ago, the Kestner factory has made fame for itself the world over with its popular Kestner dolls. As early as 1850 the dolls were exported to the United States, and are now recognized as one of the leading lines in this country.

Early in its history the Kestner factory started the home industry system, having workmen with homes in neighboring villages furnish various doll parts to be assembled at the main factory.

In 1860 a porcelain factory was acquired at Ohrdruf, making the plant complete in every respect for the manufacture of all kinds of dolls. Thus the Kestner factory is the only one where complete dolls are manufactured, as other factories have to secure the porcelain heads, etc., from porcelain manufacturers.

The factory is now operated by the grandson of the founder, and employs nearly a thousand workers, inclusive of home operators, to manufacture the enormous output.

The main product consists of kid dolls, with and without joints, extra fine jointed dolls, bisque and celluloid doll heads, bisque babies, toy, tea, dinner and toilet sets, figures, busts, etc.

In making kid dolls, the sheepskins while moist are first tightly stretched on long tables, in order to get their full surface. The skins are then given to experienced cutters, who cut by tin patterns the bodies, arms and legs, and these are subsequently deftly sewed together on machines. Stuffers then fill the bodies thus sewed together with sawdust, cork or hair.

The jointed dolls require hollow moulds, the pieces being made in two parts of paper pulp, which are fastened together and provided with the necessary sockets for ball joints. After this a flesh color is poured over them and they are put on sticks to dry before being varnished. The finished bodies and legs are turned over to joiners, who fasten heads, arms and legs together by means of rubber cords and hooks in the bodies.

Practically the same process is followed out in making the so-called patent head of paper pulp. After these are dried they are given to artists, who paint in eyes, eyebrows, hair, mouth and color the cheeks true to life. A coat of dull varnish as a finishing touch is added.

Bisque doll heads, which are usually attached to kid bodies and jointed dolls, are made in a slightly different manner. First an expert modeler makes a head of clay, and from this a number of plaster moulds are made. Into these moulds is poured a thick liquid porcelain, the preparation of which requires especial care and experience. After standing for about ten minutes, the liquid begins to harden, next the moulds, and the superfluous part is poured off. After another fifteen minutes the head is hard enough to remove from the mould, which is in two pieces that have simply to be separated. The seams on the doll head caused by the fitting together of the two parts of the mould are then smoothed down, and eyes and mouth openings are cut out and sometimes teeth set in. When the heads are throughly dried they are put in Chamotte vessels and upon porcelain supports pass into a large round kiln, where they are fired in white heat.

When placed in the hands of skilled artists for finishing up they are simply dull white porcelain. A flesh color is deftly applied, and when this is dry, cheeks, lips, eyelashes and brows are painted in.

The heads are then fired to burn the colors in.

After the colors are burned in, the heads are ready for eyes and hair. The former are inserted to stay open with cement, or for sleeping dolls they are connected with a balancing weight. A cardboard cap is inserted on the top to which the wig is to be affixed.

Celluloid doll heads at the Kestner factory are manufactured by a special process fully protected by patents. These heads are exceptionally well made, and are in great demand. When brought from the moulds smooth and shiny they are worked in such a mannner they acquire a dull, lifelike flesh tint vastly different from the usual glossy appearance of the celluloid heads coated with aniline colors, which after a short time fade and give the doll a dead expression. The Kestner heads will stand exposure to strong light, and can scarcely be distinguished from the finest bisque head.

The making of the wigs is an important factor. Human hair, or hair of the Angora goat, is wound on threads in equal lengths thus forming the so-called "Tresse", which is sewed skillfully upon a gauze cap big enough to cover the head in order to be combed, curled and trimmed with ribbon bows. The manufacture of these wigs requires special skill, and only experienced hands can be entrusted with it.

Waltershausen, the birthplace of the thousands of Kestner dolls, shipped annually to the United States, is a quaint little city of the dukedom Sachsen-Coburg-Gotha, and is beautifully situated at the foot of the Thuringian forest. It is a very industrious center, furnishing the world with various toys and useful articles. Ohrdruf, where the porcelain parts are manufactured, is located on the Ohra, about one and a half hours from Waltershausen. It is here in 724 that Bonifacius, the apostle of Germany, erected a Monastery, it being the first settlement of Christianity in Thuringia. The Michaelsi Church now stands on the site of the Monastery. For the tourist who happens to wander into these little cities there are many things quaintly historic to interest him.

Johannes Daniel Kestner first made buttons and slates of papier-mache in a factory at Waltershausen, Thur and when these lines were not successful, he began making doll bodies, using the same lathes. This was in 1804 and, in essence, became the founder of the Waltershausen doll industry and by 1906 employed close to 1000 workers.

The Kestner company made all kinds of dolls and doll bodies. They made entire dolls (one of the few German companies that did) and as early as 1845, their dolls were on either kid, muslin bodies or had wooden limbs, and papier-mache heads. By 1860 they had purchased a porcelain factory in Ohrdruf, Thur and were making their own china and bisque heads. They also made wax heads, worked in leather, cardboard and celluloid. By 1893, Kestner Company had several patents but the best known one is for their "Excelsior" bodies. Patent #70685, which is a jointed composition body. In 1895 Kestner Company registered their trademark of a crown/streamers in the United States and in 1896, in Germany.

Kestner was one firm who made "Kewpie" (1913) and in 1914 made their most famous baby "Hilda". Their next famous is the "Gibson Girl" created by Charles Dana Gibson.

During 1915 the Kestner Company registered two crown trademarks in Germany. One carries the words "Kronen Puppe" and the other "Crown Doll/Kestner/GERMANY" and after World War 1, in 1924, they made the Bye-Lo baby doll heads for Grace S. Putnam/George Borgfelt & Co.

The Ladies Home Journal had a series of paper dolls created by Sheila Young called "Lettie Lane" and in 1911 "Lettie Lane" introduced her doll "Daisy". The only way to get the doll was to sell three subscriptions, at least one renewal and two new ones, plus $4.50. The promotion included doll and patterns that followed the paper dolls. In April 1911 "Lettie Lane's Most Beautiful Doll as a Bride", July 1911, "Lettie Lane's Doll in Vacation Clothes". October 1911, "Lettie Lane's Doll in Her School Clothes" and December 1911 "Lettie Lane's Most Beautiful Doll in her Party Clothes".

The first order for the dolls was 5,000 but they were gone in a short time and 2 factories had to be used for a total of 26,000 additional dolls before the close of the offer, in January 1912. The "Lettie Lane" paper doll's "real live doll" was at first, a Kestner 174 and also used was the Kestner 171. Some of them were made by Simon & Halbig for Heinrich Handwerck (Bebe Cosmopolite) and many were from the Armand Marseille factory. A total of 31,000 "Daisy's" found their way into the hands of American children over a period of only 9 months.

Most Kestner dolls are marked with sizes that include a letter and a number. For example C-7, F-10, D-8 and some carry a mold number along with these, for example F MADE IN GERMANY 10/169. Often the J.D.K. is incised also. The most "common" mold numbers of Kestner dolls found are 154 & 171.

Adolf Kestner, during the early part of this Century, liked to refer to himself as "King" of the toy industry and due, also, to the crown seal he used is often referred to by collectors as "King Kestner".

"KING"

JOHANNES

DANIEL

KESTNER

1804 - 1930's

9" Beautiful figurine by J. D. Kestner. Every one is familiar with the Heubach (Gebruder) figurines and piano babies but do not know that other doll makers also made fine porcelain pieces. See the mark on this beautiful, rare piece in next photo. (Author).

9" - E - G

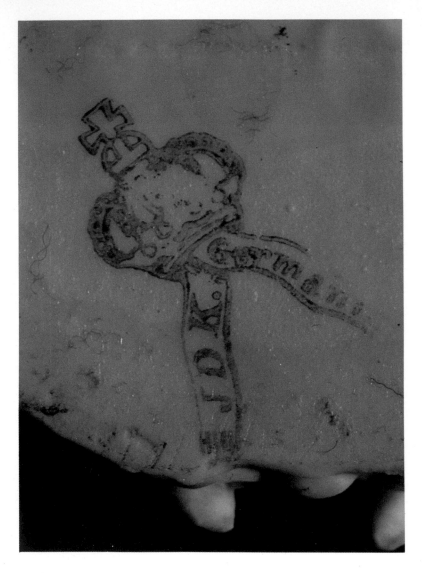

Crown and streamer mark of J. D. Kestner which was registered in 1896, found on base of figurine.

17" Shoulder head on kid body with bisque lower arms. Sleep eyes. Open mouth. MARKS: B GERMANY 6. Courtesy Kathy Walter.

19" - E - F

13" Socket head on fully jointed composition body. Open mouth/2 teeth. Set
eyes. MARKS: B MADE IN 6/ GERMANY.
Courtesy Kathy Walter.
22" - C - D

15" Shoulder head on kid body with bisque forearms. Closed mouth. MARKS: MADE IN/D GERMANY 8/. Courtesy Jay Minter.

15" J - K

18½" Turned shoulder head. Kidoline body with bisque forearms. Sleep eyes. Open mouth. MARKS: G/MADE IN GERMANY. Courtesy Kathy Walter.
16" - E - F

15" Shoulder head on kid body with bisque lower arms. Open/closed mouth. Set eyes. MARKS: 4/MADE IN GERMANY. Courtesy Kathy Walter.
15" - G - H

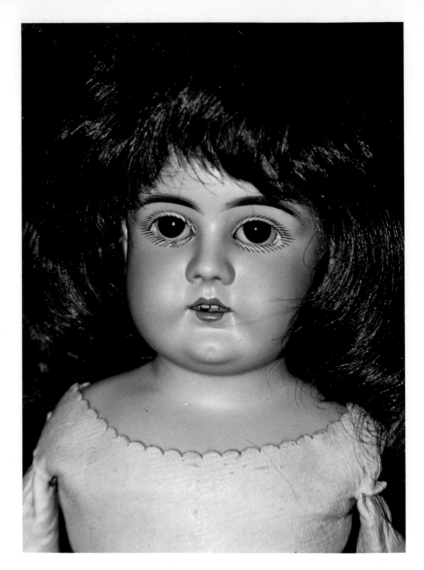

18½"Shoulder head on kid body with bisque lower arms. Sleep eyes. Open mouth with modeled teeth. MARKS: 7½/B GERMANY. Courtesy Kimport Dolls.

19" C - D

20½″ Socket head on bisque shoulder plate. Closed mouth. Probable Kestner. MARKS: 10. Courtesy Kathy Walter.
21″ H - I

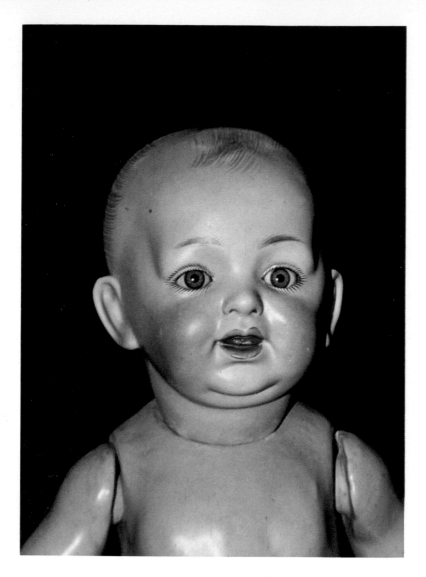

15″ Socket head on 5 piece bent leg baby body. Sleep eyes. Open mouth with 2 painted upper teeth. MARKS: J.D.K./12/ MADE IN GERMANY. Courtesy Kimport Dolls.

15″ E - F

17" Shoulder head on kid body with bisque lower arms. Open mouth. MARKS: 5-143. Courtesy Kathy Walter.
17" F - G

10½" Shoulder head on kid body with bisque forearms. Open/ closed mouth MARKS: 145. Courtesy Kathy Walter.
11" - A - B

18" Shoulder head on kid body with bisque lower arms. Open mouth. MARKS: 7 ½ / 148. Courtesy Kimport Dolls.
18" C - D

20½" Shoulder head on kid body with bisque forearms. Sleep eyes. Open mouth. MARKS 8/148/MADE IN GERMANY. Courtesy Kathy Walter.
21" C - D

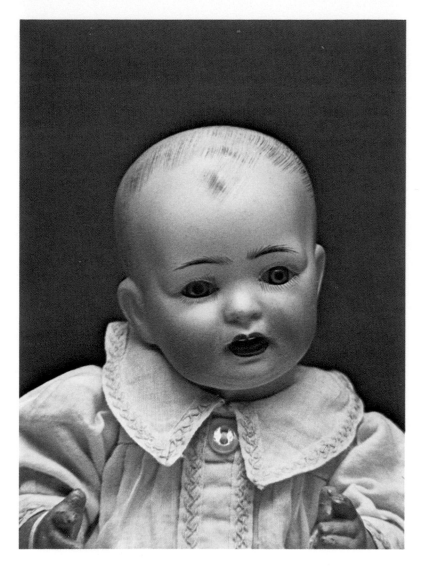

14" Socket head on 5 piece bent leg baby
body. Open mouth with two upper teeth
and molded tongue. Brush stroke hair.
MARKS: MADE IN GERMANY 151. Courtesy Kimport Dolls.
14" E - F

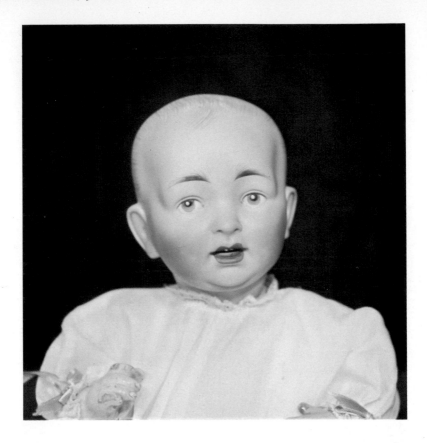

12" Socket head on 5 piece bent leg baby body. Mauve tinted intaglio eyes. Brush painted hair. Open mouth/2 upper teeth and molded tongue. Dimples in cheeks. Red lines above eyes and in top groove of ears. MARKS: MADE IN GERMANY 151/5. Courtesy Jeanne Gregg.
12" D - E

9" Socket head on 5 piece bent leg baby body. Open/closed mouth with two upper teeth. Brush painted hair. MARKS: MADE IN GERMANY 151/5. Courtesy Jeanne Gregg.

9" E - F

12½" Shoulder head on kid body with bisque lower arms. "Fly away" type eyebrows. Open mouth with set in teeth. Painted lashes below eyes only. MARKS: DEP 154.1. Courtesy Kathy Walter.
13" - A - B

17" Shoulder head on kid body with bisque lower arms. Open mouth with modeled in teeth. Lashes painted over & under eyes. MARKS: 5 3/4 154 DEP. Courtesy Kathy Walter.

26" - D - E

16" Socket head on fully jointed composition body. Open mouth. Pierced ears.
MARKS: F½ MADE IN 6½/GERMANY
167. Courtesy Kimport Dolls.
16" - C - D

16" Socket head on fully jointed composition body. Closed mouth. Sleep eyes.
MARKS: B½ MADE IN 6½/GERMANY/
169. BODY: GERMANY. Courtesy Kimport Dolls.   1
                16" - K -L

21" Socket head on fully jointed composition body. Open mouth. Sleep eyes.
Lettie Lanes's "Daisy". Refer to Series
1-page 158. MARKS: F MADE IN 10/171.
Courtesy Kimport Dolls.
21" C - D

12½" Ball (bald) shoulder head on fashion type kid body. Bisque lower arms. Closed mouth. Set eyes. Pierced ears. MARKS: 172, a known Kestner number. Courtesy Kathy Walter.

13" - E - F

19" Celluloid shoulder head with kid body. Set eyes/lashes open mouth. MARKS: J.D.K./201/4. Body marked: J.D.K. GERMANY / ½ CORK STUFFED. Courtesy Kathy Walter.

19" - C -D

17" Socket head on 5 piece bent leg baby
body. Open mouth. Sleep eyes. 2 lower
teeth. MARKS: MADE IN GERMANY/211
Courtesy Jeanne Gregg.
17" E - F

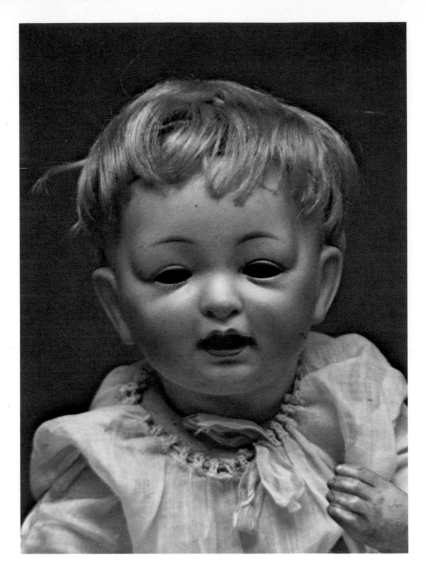

12″ Socket head on 5 piece bent leg baby body.
Open/closed mouth. Brown sleep eyes.
MARKS: ℱ   MADE IN 10/GERMANY/
211/J.D.K.   Courtesy Kimport Dolls.
12″ D-E.

21" Socket head on fully jointed composition body. Fur eyebrows. Open mouth.
MARKS: MADE IN 9/GERMANY J.D.K./
215. Courtesy Jay Minter.
21" - E - F

18" Socket head on 5 piece bent leg baby body. Open mouth with modeled tongue. Set eyes. MARKS: J.D.K./236. Courtesy Kimport Dolls.

18" F - G

14" Socket head on 5 piece bent leg baby
body. Open mouth. MARKS: G MADE IN
GERMANY/11/245 J.D.K. Jr./ 1914
HILDA. Courtesy Jeanne Gregg
14"-J-K

10" Socket head on 5 piece bent leg baby
body. Open mouth. MARKS: GERMANY/
J.D.K./257. Courtesy Kimport Dolls.
10" - E - F

MADE IN GERMANY A KESTNER	Shoulder head. Open mouth. 19" E - F
A GERMANY 5	Shoulder head. Open/closed mouth. 23" G - H
B MADE IN GERMANY Excelsior, on body DRP No. 70686 Germany	Socket head. Open mouth. Ca. 1896. 22" C - D
⟨K⟩ GERMANY CENTURY	Made for Century Doll Co. Flanged closed dome, closed mouth. 15" E - F
JDK KESTNER	Oriental socket head. Open mouth. 14" L - M
JDK C.M. BERGMANN	Made for C. M. Bergmann. Socket head. Open mouth. 26" D - E
JDK (turtlemark)	Bisque head on celluloid body by Rheinische Gummi Co. 18" I - J
1 Copy by Grace S. Putnam Germany	All bisque. One piece body & head. 1923. 6" D - E
JDK 3 4/0	Socket head. Painted eyes. 8" A - B
MADE IN L GERMANY 3	Shoulder head. Open/closed mouth with modeled teeth. 23" G - H
6-12 Copr. GRACE S. PUTNAM GERMANY	Bye-lo baby. 1927. 16" F - G
MADE IN D GERMANY 8	Socket head. Open mouth. 14" B - C
MADE IN JDK GERMANY 8	Turned shoulder head. Open mouth. 19" E - F

KESTNER, J.D.

MADE IN **E GERMANY 9**	Socket head. Open mouth. 1892. 26″ E - F
H½ GERMANY	Shoulder head. Open mouth. 23″ F - G
JDK 10 **GERMANY**	Socket head. Closed mouth. 1912. 18″ H - I
JDK **MADE IN GERMANY 10**	Socket head. Open/closed mouth with two lower teeth. 12″ G - H
MADE IN **G GERMANY 11**	Brown socket head. Open mouth. 16″ E - F
JDK 11 **MADE IN GERMANY**	Socket head. Open/closed mouth. Painted eyes to side. 11″ C - D
CENTURY DOLL CO **KESTNER** **GERMANY** **12**	Made for Century Doll Co. Shoulder head. Open/closed mouth. Molded hair. 21″ F - G
JDK **HANDWERCK H 12**	Made for Heinrich Handwerck. Socket head. Open mouth. C - D
MADE IN **H GERMANY 12** **JDK**	Socket head. Open/closed mouth. 1892. 23″ G - H
Ges Gesch O'Neill **JDK 12**	Socket head. Closed mouth. 1913. 6″ A - B
JDK 13 **MADE IN GERMANY**	Socket head. Open mouth. 18″. B - C
I GERMANY 13	Socket head. Open mouth. 16″ B - C
MADE IN **I GERMANY 13** **JDK**	Socket head. Open mouth. 1892. 26″ C - D

J GERMANY 13

Socket head. Open mouth. 1896. 27" F - G

KK GERMANY 14½

Socket head. Open mouth. 1896. 26" E - F

INCIDEIN
L GERMANY 15

Socket head. Open mouth. 23" C - D

JDK
INCIDEIN 15 GERMANY

Socket head. Open mouth. 23" C - D

MADE IN
L GERMANY 15

Socket head. Closed mouth. 21" J - K

MADE IN
L GERMANY 15

Socket head (swivel) on shoulder plate. Closed mouth. 21" J - K

MADE IN
L½ GERMANY 15½

Socket head. Closed mouth. 14" I - J

JDK
MADE IN GERMANY
16

Socket head. Open mouth. 21" C - D

MADE IN GERMANY 16
GES. NO. 1 GESCH.
16/OZ

Shoulder head. Open/closed mouth with two teeth. Painted eyes. Molded blond boy's hairdo. 16" I - J

MADE IN
M½ GERMANY 16½
Excelsior (on body)

Socket head. Open mouth. 1892. 14" B - C

MADE IN
N GERMANY 17

Socket head. Open mouth. 1892. 17" C - D

20   10
COPR BY
GRACE S PUTNAM
GERMANY

All bisque. One piece body & head. Painted eyes. 6" D - E

K & CO.
JDK
MADE IN GERMANY
26   81

Socket head. Open mouth. 16" C - D

JDK 47
MADE IN GERMANY

Socket head. Open mouth. 12" A - B

JDK
48
MADE IN GERMANY

Socket head. Open mouth. 16" B - C

MADE IN GERMANY
GES. NO. 116 GESCH
16/0
Crown seal (on body)

Shoulder head. Open/closed mouth with two teeth. Painted eyes. Molded hair & bonnet. 18" E - F

JDK 117
GERMANY

Socket head. Open mouth. 16" E - F

MAE IN
JDK GERMANY 123

Socket head. Open/closed mouth. Molded hair. 18" H - I

MADE IN
L GERMANY 15
128

Socket head. Closed mouth. 1892. 16" I - J

MADE IN
H GERMANY 12
129

Socket head (swivel) on shoulder plate. Open mouth. 1892. 18" D - E

MADE IN
H GERMANY 12
129

Socket head. Open mouth. 21" D - E

MADE IN
K GERMANY 135

Turned shoulder head. Open mouth. 25" D - E

136 10

Socket head. Open mouth. 26" C - D

7 137 DEP
Crown seal (on body)

Shoulder head. Open mouth. 16" B - C

139 26 H

Shoulder head. Open mouth. 18" B - C

MADE IN
L GERMANY 15
141

Socket head. Open mouth. Ca. 1892. 21" C - D

JDK 142	Socket head. Closed mouth. 14" H - I
MADE IN O GERMANY 18 142	Socket head. Open mouth. 16" D - E
C GERMANY 3 KESTNER 143	Socket head. Open mouth 19" F - G
143 4/0	Shoulder head. Open mouth. 18" F - G
JDK - 145	Socket head. Closed mouth. 11" A - B
JDK 146	Socket head (swivel) on shoulder plate. Open mouth. 25" F - G
K GERMANY 146	Socket head. Open mouth. 18" E - F
JDK 147	Turned shoulder head. Open mouth. 25" D - E
MADE IN GERMANY 2 148	Shoulder head. Open mouth. 26" C - D
150.1	All bisque. Some have Kestner seal on body. 8" A - B
GERMANY 151	Socket head. Open mouth. 16" C - D
MADE IN GERMANY 151 2	Socket head. Open/closed mouth. Two teeth, tongue and molded hair. 16" F - G
C 151 GERMANY 7	Socket head with closed dome. Open mouth. 16" D - E
MADE IN GERMANY 151 5	Socket head. Open mouth. 18" E - F
MADE IN GERMANY 152 1	Socket head. Open mouth. 20" F - G
JDK 152/5 MADE IN GERMANY	Socket head. Open/closed mouth. 20" G - H
L.W. & CO. 12 152	Made for Louis Wolf & Co. in 1916. Socket head. Open mouth. 20" F - G

KESTNER, J.D.

154   DEP
Crown seal (on body)

Shoulder head. Open mouth. 12″ A - B

D DEP 9
154

Socket head. Open mouth. 26″ D - E

MADE IN
B GERMANY 6
155

Socket head. Open mouth. 16″ C - D

MADE IN GERMANY
J 3/4 DEP   13 3/4
156

Socket head. Open mouth. 26″ D - E

KESTNER 158

Socket head. Open mouth. 30″ F - G

158 5/0

All bisque. One piece body & head. Closed mouth. Painted eyes. 8″ B - C

MADE IN
C GERMANY 7
160

Socket head. Open mouth. 28″ G - H

MADE IN
A GERMANY 5
161

Socket head. Open mouth. 16″ D - E

MADE IN
L GERMANY 13
162

Socket head. Open mouth. 14″ D - E

21
164
GERMANY 34

Oriental socket head. Open mouth. 16″ L - M

MADE IN
C GERMANY 7
164

Socket head (swivel) on shoulder plate. Open mouth. 32″ F - G

MADE IN
L½ GERMANY 15½
164

Socket head. Open mouth. 12″ A - B

JDK 165

Socket head. Smile closed mouth. Googly eyes. 16″ Z

9.
166
E MADE IN GERMANY

Shoulder head. Open mouth. 26" F - G

MADE IN
B GERMANY 6
167

Socket head. Open mouth. 14" C - D

MADE IN
H½ GERMANY 12½
167

Socket head. Closed mouth. 26" K - L

MADE IN
C GERMANY 7
168

Socket head. Open mouth. 26" D - E

MADE IN
C GERMANY 7
169

Socket head. Closed mouth. 21" K - L

DK 169

Socket head. Open mouth. 21" E - F

MADE IN
3½ GERMANY 6½
171

Socket head. Open mouth. 12" B - C

MADE IN GERMANY
171 GERMANY 10½

Shoulder head. Open mouth. 26" D - E

NCIDEIN F½
171 GERMANY 15/0

Socket head. Open mouth. 26" D - E

172
MADE IN GERMANY
Crown seal (on body)

Shoulder head. Closed mouth. Gibson Girl.
14" M - N

DK 172

Socket head. Open mouth. 14" E - F

MADE IN
3 GERMANY 6
74

Socket head. Open mouth. 26" F - G

80   12/0x
Crown seal (on body)

Socket head. Open mouth. 16" C - D

KESTNER 182	Socket head. Open mouth. 14" C - D
MADE IN B GERMANY 6 186	Socket head. Open/closed mouth. Teeth. Painted eyes. 1910. 23" G - H
MADE IN H GERMANY 12 187	Socket head. Closed mouth. 18" J - K
B½ GERMANY 6½ 189	Socket head. Closed mouth. 16" J - K
JDK 192 GERMANY	Socket head. Open mouth. (Jumeau Body). 21" H - I
MADE IN D GERMANY 8 193	Socket head. Open mouth. 16" D - E
MADE IN GERMANY D 195	Socket head. Open mouth. Fur eyebrows. 23" E - F
195 DEP 6 Crown seal (on body)	Shoulder head. Open mouth. 23" E - F
KESTNER ROYAL 195 DEP 10 F MADE IN GERMANY	Shoulder head. Open mouth. 16" D - E
MADE IN H GERMANY 12 196	Socket head. Open mouth. 21" C - D
JDK 200 Turtlemark	Celluloid socket head. Ca. 1924. 19" C - D
C.P. 201	Made for Carl Trautman of Catterfelde Puppenfabrik. Socket head. Open/closed mouth. Painted eyes. 16" G - H
J.D.K. 201 GERMANY	Shoulder head. Open mouth. 18" D -

J.D.K. 201 7
Crown seal (on body)

Celluloid socket head. Closed mouth. 18" C - D

JDK 201

Celluloid shoulder head. Open mouth. 23" C - D

MADE IN GERMANY
BISCUIT BABIES
1/12 203 D3
(see page 53 for drawings)

Socket head. Closed mouth. 12" G - H

F GERMANY 10
211 JDK

Socket head. Open mouth. 1910. 13" D - E

MADE IN
J GERMANY 13
211

Socket head. Open/closed mouth. Two lower teeth. 13" G - H

JDK 214
GERMANY

Socket head (swivel) on shoulder plate. Open mouth. 27" F - G

MADE IN
K GERMANY 14
215
JDK

Socket head. Open mouth. 21" E - F

MADE IN GERMANY
GES 216 GESCH

Shoulder head. Open/closed mouth. Two lower teeth. Painted eyes. 16" G - H

JDK 216

Socket head. Open mouth. 18" C - D

217 A
KESTNER

All bisque. Closed smile mouth. Googlie painted eyes. 12" K - L

MADE IN
Q GERMANY 20
JDK 220

Socket head. Open mouth. 20" E - F

GERMANY
JDK 221
GES. GESCH.

Socket head. Closed smile mouth. Googlie eyes. 16" V - W

MADE IN
F GERMANY 10
226
J.D.K.

Socket head. Open mouth. 1896. 14" D - E

Turtle mark
MADE IN
C GERMANY 7
JDK
226

Celluloid socket head. Open mouth. 16" B - C

JDK 234
GERMANY

Shoulder head. Open mouth. 18" C - D

MADE IN GERMANY
JDK
235

Shoulder head. Open mouth. 16" C - D

J.D.K. 236

Socket head. Open mouth. 18" F - G

JDK 237
GERMANY

Socket head. Open mouth. After 1910. 16" C - D

MADE IN
G GERMANY 11
237   15
JDK Jr. 1914 HILDA
GES GESCH N 1070

Socket head. Open mouth. 20" K - I

JDK
241
GERMANY

Socket head. Open mouth. 16" D - E

MADE IN
A GERMANY 5
243
JDK

Olive socket head. Slant sleep eyes. Open mouth. 16" K - L

MADE IN
G GERMANY 11
243
JDK

Olive socket head. Open/closed mouth. 16" M - N

HILDA
MADE IN
N GERMANY 16
JDK 1914
5 Gesch N 1070
245

Socket head. Open mouth. 14" J - K

JDK 247
GERMANY

Socket head. Open/closed mouth. 16" I - J

247   6/0
GERMANY

Bisculine socket head. Open mouth. 14" B - C

MADE IN GERMANY
JDK 249

Socket head. Open mouth. 16" C - D

MADE IN GERMANY
JDK
257
27

Socket head. Open mouth. 1914. 20" F - G

JDK
260
GERMANY
34
37 - 40

Socket head. Open mouth. 1919. 20" G - H

JDK 261
GERMANY

Celluloid shoulder head. Open mouth. 18" C - D

Scroll (see introduction)
262   30 - 31
MADE IN GERMANY

Socket head. Open mouth. 1912. 26" F - G

K & CO.
CATTERFELDER
PUPPENFABRIK
264
2

Made for Catterfelder Puppenfabrik. Open/closed mouth. Socket head. 18" G - H

C.P.
270
39

Made for Carl Trautman. Socket head. Open mouth. 38" H - I

KESTNER, J.D.

SIEGFRIED
MADE IN GERMANY
272

Flange neck head. Closed mouth. 21" F - G

295 2 H

Socket head. Open mouth. 12" B - C

MADE IN GERMANY
401 H 6/0

Shoulder head. Open/closed mouth. Closed dome. Painted eyes. 12" B - C

COPR BY
GRACE S PUTNAM
518
GERMANY

Made for George Borgfeltd. 1923. All bisque Bye-lo baby. 26" D - E

639
GERMANY
6

Turned shoulder head. Closed dome. Closed mouth. 18" G - H

MADE IN GERMANY
JDK 920

Socket head. Open mouth. 16" C - D

KEWPIE
ROSE O'NEILL
10 954 GERMANY

1913. All bisque. 8" A - B

SIMON

&

HALBIG

1870 - 1930's

THE SIMON & HALBIG STORY

The Simon & Halbig firm operated from sometime in the late 1860's or early 1870's until 1930's.

Some Simon & Halbig dolls have molded hair and untinted bisque and quite a few are found that have ball (bald) heads, generally the lady types, that were so popular in the mid 1879's. Simon & Halbig was one of the largest German firms and supplied many heads/designs to French doll makers during the years of the 1870's and the 1880's.

In 1890 they obtained patents for movable eyes. One was a wire with a loop, through a hole in the back of the head and later a wire with a handle to make the eyes move from right to left. They made dolls for many companies which included: Fleischman & Blodel, Gimbel Bros., Jumeau, Kammer & Reinhardt, Heinrich Handwerck, C.M. Bergman, Cuno & Otto Dressel, Bawo & Dotter, Hamberger Co., George Borgfelt and others.

In 1895 Simon left the firm (retired or deceased) and Carl Halbig took over as a single owner. Carl Halbig did not register "S & H" until 1905.

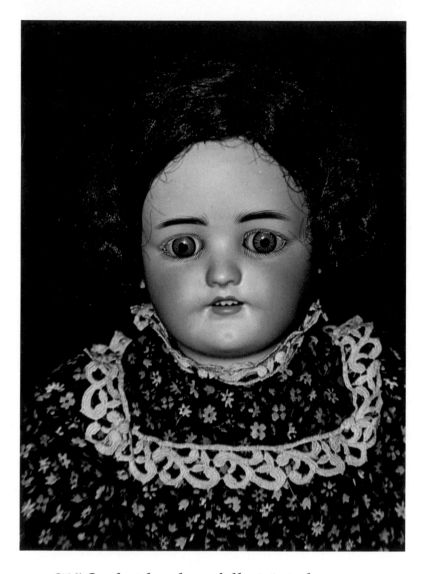

21" Socket head on fully jointed composition body. Sleep eyes. Open mouth.
MARKS: 550/GERMANY/SIMON & HAL-
BIG. Courtesy Kathy Walters.
21" - C - D

18″ Socket head on composition body with straight wrists. Closed mouth. Ears pierced above earlobe into head. Ball (bald) head with 1 hole. MARKS: S 11 H 719 DEP. High on head. Original. Author. 18″ I - J

25"Socket head on fully jointed composition body. Set eyes. Closed mouth.
Pierced ears. MARKS: S 13 H/939.
Courtesy Helen Draves.
25" K - L

8″ Shoulder head on cloth body with
bisque arms. Sleep eyes. Closed mouth.
Ca.1890. MARKS: SH 4/0 950. Original
clothes. Courtesy Kimport Dolls.
8″ - D - E

19½" Shoulder head on kid body with bisque lower arms. Open mouth. Paperweight set eyes. Pierced ears. MARKS: S & H 1010. Courtesy Kathy Walter.
20" D - E

19½" Shoulder head on kid body with bisque lower arms. Pierced ears. Open mouth. Set eyes. MARKS: S 7 H 1010 DEP. Courtesy Kathy Walter.
20" D - E

16" Brown bisque socket head on fully
jointed composition body. Large sleep
brown eyes. Open mouth. Original Hindu
costume. MARKS: SH. 1039/6 DEP.
Courtesy Kimport Dolls.
16" I - J

32" Socket head on fully jointed composition body. Set eyes. Open mouth.
MARKS: 1078/SIMON & HALBIG/S &
H/ 17. Courtesy Jay Minter.
32" F -G

10" Socket head on 5 piece heavy composition body. Blue sleep eyes. Open mouth. Modeled on heeled shoes. MARKS: 1078/SIMON & HALBIG/S & H. Courtesy Kathy Walter.
10" B - C

Shows body of 10" 1078.

29" Shoulder head on kid/muslin body with bisque lower arms. Set eyes. Open mouth. MARKS: S&H 1079. Courtesy Kimport Dolls.

29" F - G

18" Turned shoulder head on kid body with bisque arms. Open mouth with modeled teeth. " sew holes front & back. MARKS: GERMANY / SIMON & HALBIG / 1080 S & H 7. Courtesy Jay Minter.
18" D - E

13" Socket head on fully jointed compo-
sition body. Sleep almond shaped eyes.
Olive skin tones. Pierced ears. MARKS:
SH-1129 / DEP./3/ GERMANY. Courtesy
Kimport Dolls.

13" L -M

25" Socket head on adult composition
body. Open mouth. Pierced ears. MARKS:
1159. Courtesy Helen Draves.
25" J - K

24" Shoulder head on kid body with
bisque forearms. Open mouth. MARKS:
1260 GERMANY DEP/ _N_ 12. Courtesy
Kathy Walter.
24"-E-F

15½" Socket head on fully jointed composition/wood body. Pierced ears, open mouth & sleep eyes. All original. MARKS: 1329/GERMANY/SIMON & HALBIG/S&H/4. Courtesy Kimport Dolls.

16" M-N

25" Socket head on fully jointed spring strung composition body. Set eyes. Modeled Eyebrows. Pierced ears. Open mouth. ORIGINAL MARKS: C.M. BERGMANN/SIMON HALBIG 11. Courtesy Jeanne Gregg.
25" D - E

29" Socket head on fully jointed composition body. Sleep eyes. Modeled eyebrows. Open mouth. Pierced ears.
MARKS: HEINRICH HANDWERCK SIM-
ON HALBIG 5. Courtesy Jeanne Gregg.
29" E - F

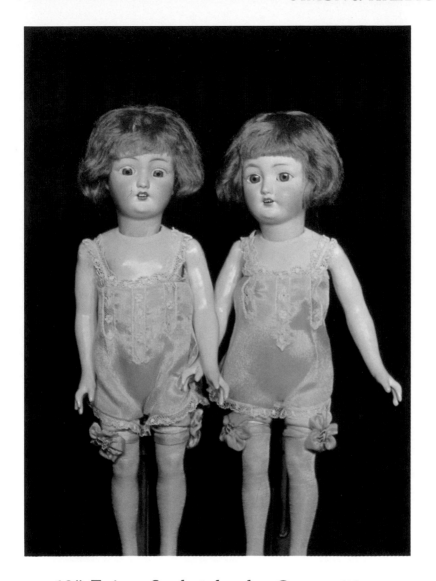

13" Twins. Socket heads. Composition body with straight arms. Legs jointed above knees. Sleep eyes. Original Teddies, garters, silk stockings and patent shoes. MARKS: S & H 5. Childhood dolls of Jeanne Gregg and sister.

13" C - D

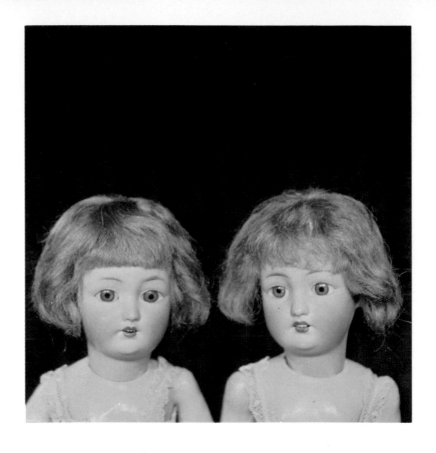

A closer look at the heads of the S & H twins.

18″ Socket head. Key wind mechanical walker. Flirty sleep eyes. Pierced ears. MARKS: S & H 7½. Courtesy Jeanne Gregg.

18″ H - I

Shows body and key of mechanical walker.

16½" Socket head on fully jointed composition body. Sleep eyes. Pierced ears.
Open mouth. MARKS: SIMON HALBIG
K △ R/43. Courtesy Kathy Walter.
16½"C - D

19" Socket head on toddler body. Flirty sleep eyes. Open mouth with 2 upper teeth and tremble tongue. MARKS: K   R SIMON HALBIG 126. Courtesy Jeanne Gregg.

19" F - G

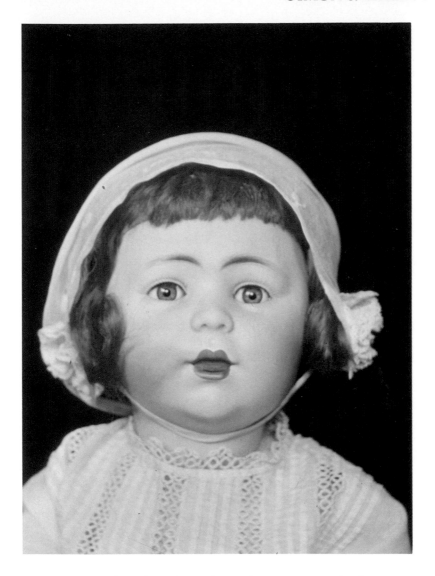

22" Socket head on bent leg 5 piece baby body. Sleep eyes. Open mouth. MARKS: JUTTA/1914/12. Made by Simon & Halbig for Cuno Otto Dressel. Childhood doll of Jeanne Gregg.
22" E - F

CMB S & H 3 / 0	Made for C.M. Bergmann. Socket head. Op mouth. 18″ B - C
SIMON & HALBIG S & H 8 / 0	Socket head. Open mouth 10″ H -
GERMANY HEINRICH HANDWERCK SIMON & HALBIG 1	Made for Heinrich Handwerck. Ca. 189 Socket head. Open mouth. 16″ C -
S & H 3	All bisque. Closed mouth, inset eyes. Model on shoes. 6″. B - C
S & H CMB 3	Made for C.M. Bergmann. Socket head. Op mouth. 26″ C - D
C M BERGMANN Simon & Halbig 3 ½	Made for C.M. Bergmann. Socket hea Open mouth. 18″ B - C
GERMANY HANDWERCK HALBIG 4	Made for Heinrich Handwerck. Socket hea Open mouth. 26″ D - E
HALBIG C M BERGMANN S & H 5	Made for C.M. Bergmann. Ca. 1895. Sock head. Open mouth. 30″ E - F
C M BERGMANN SIMON & HALBIG 6	Made for C.M. Bergmann. Ca. 1897. Sock head. Open mouth 12″ A - B
HEINRICH HANDWERCK SIMON & HALBIG 7 BEBE COSMOPOLITE (body)	Made for Heinrich Handwerck. In 189 Socket head. Open mouth. 16″ C -

GERMANY SIMON & HALBIG S & H 9	Socket head. Open mouth 26" C - D
GERMANY HALBIG S & H 10	Socket head. Open mouth. Ca. 1895. 16" C - D
S & H 10½	Socket head. Open mouth. Flirty sleep eyes. 18" D - F
SH/AW 13	Made for Adolf Wislizenus. Socket head. Open mouth. 21" C - D
HALBIG K*R 15	Made for Kammer & Reinhardt. Ca. 1897. Socket head. Open mouth. 22" C - D
SH 15 DEP.	Socket head. Open mouth. 22" C - D
L SIMON & HALBIG K*R 30	Made for Kammer & Reinhardt in 1902. Socket head. Box with three extra heads. 12" F - G
SIMON & HALBIG K*R GERMANY 39	Made for Kammer & Reinhardt in 1905. Socket head. Open mouth 17" C - D
SIMON & HALBIG K*R GERMANY48	Made for Kammer & Reinhardt. Ca. 1905. Socket head. Open mouth. 27" D - E
K*R SIMON & HALBIG 50	Made for Kammer & Reinhardt. Ca. 1900. Socket head. Open mouth. 14" C - D
SIMON & HALBIG 50 11	Shoulder head. Closed mouth. 16" J - K
SIMON & HALBIG K*R 53	Made for Kammer & Reinhardt. Brown bisque socket head. Closed mouth. 16" J - K

SIMON & HALBIG
K * R
GERMANY
68

Made for Kammer & Reinhardt. Called "The Flirt". 1908. Socket head. Flirty sleep eyes. Eyelids move with eyes. 16" F - G

HALBIG
K * R
70

Made for Kammer & Reinhardt. Ca. 1896. Socket head. Open mouth. 25" F - G

SIMON & HALBIG
K * R
GERMANY 85

Made for Kammer & Reinhardt. 1905. Socket head. Open mouth. 18" D - E

11½ 99
HANDWERCK
HALBIG
GERMANY

Made for Heinrich Handwerck. 1899. Socket head. Open mouth. 16" C - D

SIMON & HALBIG
S & C
100
GERMANY

Made for Sannier & Caut. Socket head. Open mouth. 26" F - G

SIMON & HALBIG
K * R
101

Made for Kammer & Reinhardt. Socket head. Open mouth. 16" D - E

HANDWERCK
109   11
GERMANY
HALBIG

Made for Heinrich Handwerck in 1895. Socket head. Open mouth. 23" G - H

SIMON & HALBIG
114
K * R
L

Made for Kammer & Reinhardt. Socket head. Closed mouth. 14" O - P

K * R
SIMON & HALBIG
115
60

Made for Kammer & Reinhardt in 1912. Socket head. Closed mouth. 14" O - P

K * R
SIMON & HALBIG
115a
68

Made for Kammer & Reinhardt in 1912. Socket head. Closed mouth pouty. 9" M - N

K * R
SIMON & HALBIG
116a
38

Made for Kammer & Reinhardt. Socket head. 2 teeth, tongue. 17" K - M

SIMON & HALBIG
K * R
117

Made for Kammer & Reinhardt in 1919. Socket head. Closed mouth. 18" S - T

K * R
SIMON & HALBIG
117a

Made for Kammer & Reinhardt. Socket head. Closed mouth. 23" T - U

SIMON & HALBIG
K * R
117n

Made for Kammer & Reinhardt. Socket head. Open mouth. Flirty eyes. 20" F - G

K * R
SIMON & HALBIG
118
45

Made for Kammer & Reinhardt. Socket head. Ca. 1919. 14" J - K

119   13
HANDWERCK 5
HALBIG

Made for Heinrich Handwerck. Socket head. Open mouth. 16" C - D

S H 120

Socket head. Open mouth. 28" G - H

K * R
SIMON & HALBIG
121
25

Made for Kammer & Reinhardt. Socket head. Open mouth. Ca. 1920. 12" D - E

K * R
SIMON & HALBIG
121
30

Made for Kammer & Reinhardt. 1920. Socket head. Open/closed mouth with 2 teeth. Flirty, sleep eyes. 16" J - K

K * R
SIMON & HALBIG
122
25

Made for Kammer & Reinhardt Ca. 1920.
Socket head. 14" D - E

SIMON & HALBIG
K * R
126

Made for Kammer & Reinhardt. Socket head.
Open mouth. 14" F - G

S. H. 126

Socket head. Open/closed mouth. 23" E. F

K * R
SIMON & HALBIG
127
30

Made for Kammer & Reinhardt. Socket head.
Open mouth.

K * R
 SIMON & HALBIG
128
36

Made for Kammer & Reinhardt. Socket head.
Open mouth. 26" C - D

S & H 139 DEP

Oriental. Ca. 1900 . Olive socket head. Open
mouth. 15" M - N

151 S& H
1

Socket head. Painted eyes. Open/closed
mouth ("Spinning Wheel" by Genevieve
Angione-May 1964). 16" L - M

SIMON & HALBIG
     a   h
        w
MADE IN GERMANY
156   8

Made for Adolf Hulss in 1925. Socket head.
Open mouth. 28" G - I

SIMON & HALBIG
159

Socket head. Open mouth. 16" C - D

BERGMANN
191 C.B.

Made for C.M. Bergmann. Socket head. Open
mouth. 18" C - D

K * R
SIMON & HALBIG
246
45

Made for Kammer & Reinhardt in 1900.
Shoulder head. Open mouth.

H 282 — Socket head. Open mouth. 14" C - D

H 382 — Socket head. Flapper body. 14" C - D

K * R
402 S H — Made for Kammer & Reinhardt, Socket head. Open mouth. 16" D - E

K * R
03 S H — Made for Kammer & Reinhardt. Socket head. Walker. Open mouth. 21" F - G

IMON & HALBIG
K * R
03 — Made for Kammer & Reinhardt. Socket head. Open/closed mouth. 18" K - L

K * R
IMON & HALBIG
03
2 — Made for Kammer & Reinhardt. Socket head. Open mouth. 20" E - F

& H 409 — Socket head. Open mouth. 30" G - H

H 11 461 — Socket head and shoulder plate. 16" C - D

30
ERMANY
IMON & HALBIG — Socket head. Open mouth. 21" C - D

& H
30
ERMANY
EBE COSMOPOLITE (on box) — Made for Heinrich Handwerck. 1895. Socket head. Open mouth. 16" C - D

40
ERMANY
IALBIG
& H — Socket head. Open mouth. 30" G - H

IMON & HALBIG
40 S & H
ERMANY — Socket head (swivel) on bisque shoulder plate. Open mouth. 16" D - E

550 GERMANY G SIMON & HALBIG S & H	Made for Gimbel Bros. NY. Socket head. Open mouth. 21″ C - D
SIMON & HALBIG S & H 550 13	Socket head. Open mouth. 16″ B - C
570 GERMANY HALBIG S&H	Socket head. Open mouth. Walking body, head turns. 18″ F - G
570 HALBIG S & H GERMANY	Socket head. Open mouth. 18″ D - E
SIMON & HALBIG 576 GERMANY	Socket head. Open mouth. 16″ C - D
MADE IN GERMANY SIMON & HALBIG C.M. BERGMANN 612	Made for C.M. Bergmann. Socket head. Open mouth. 16″ C - D
SIMON & HALBIG 616 MADE IN GERMANY	Flanged composition head. 1920. Open mouth. 12″ C - D
SIMON & HALBIG 670 GERMANY	Socket head. Open mouth. 16″ D - E
S & H 719 DEP	Socket head (swivel) on shoulder plate. Closed mouth. 20″ I - J
SIMON & HALBIG 719 S11H DEP	Socket head. Open mouth. 20″ E - F
S & H 7 1 9 DEP	Socket head. Closed mouth. 16″ I - J

S 5 H 739 DEP	Socket head. Open/closed mouth. 16" I - J
S 10 H 739 DEP	Brown socket head. Open mouth. 18" D - E
S 5 H 739 DEP	Brown socket head. Closed mouth. 14" I - J
S 10 H 759 DEP	Brown socket head. Open mouth. 20" D - E
S & H 769 DEP	Socket head. Closed mouth. 17" I - J
S H 905	Socket head (swivel) on shoulder plate. Closed mouth. 21" K - L
S H 908	Socket head (swivel) on shoulder plate. Closed mouth. 16" K - L
S 8 H 929 DEP	Socket head. Closed mouth. 21" K - L
S 11 H 939 DEP	Socket head. Closed mouth. 25" K - L
S 16 H 939 DEP	Socket head. Open mouth. 36" I - J
S 2 H 940	Shoulder head. Closed dome. Open/closed mouth. 26" K - L
S 2 H 940	Socket head (swivel) on shoulder plate. Open/closed mouth. 14" I - J
S 2 H 945 DEP	Socket head. Closed mouth. 16" I - J
S 1 H 949 DEP	Socket head. Closed mouth. 16" J - K
S 10 H 949	Socket head (swivel) on shoulder plate. Closed dome & mouth. 25" K - L
S 9 H 949	Socket head. Open mouth. 18" E - F
SH 2 950	Shoulder head. Closed mouth. 8" D - E
SH 959 SIMON & HALBIG 9	Socket head (swivel) on shoulder plate. Closed mouth. 26" K - L
960 S H	Socket head. Closed mouth. 18" K - L
S 2 H 1000 GERMANY SIMON & HALBIG	Socket head (swivel) on shoulder plate. Open mouth. 32" F - H

1008 SIMON & HALBIG S & H GERMANY	Socket head. Open/closed mouth. 16 I - J
S 1 H 1009 DEP st GERMANY	Brown socket head. Open mouth. 21" F - G
S 8 H 1009N DEP st GERMANY	Socket head (swivel) on shoulder plate. Open mouth. 21" F - G
S 8 H 1010 DEP	Shoulder head. Open mouth. 1880. 20" D - E
SH 1010 DEP E	Shoulder head. Open/closed mouth. Ca. 1890. 26" E - F
SH 1019 DEP GERMANY	Socket head. Open mouth. Ca. 1890. 8" A - B
1019 HALBIG S & H GERMANY 2	Made for Elie Martin. Swimming doll. Socket head. Closed mouth. Tag on body: 207188/Elie Martin/Automatic Swimming Toy/Patented August 20, 1878. 12" J - K
SH 1039 4 DEP	Hindu Socket head. Open mouth. Ca. 1890. 16" I - J
SH 1039 3 DEP	Socket head. Open mouth. 15" C - D
12 SH 1039 Wimpern Geschutt	Socket head (eyelashes) Mechanical. Marks on body: A La Tentation, Guyot Bebe & Jouets. 18" G - H
SH1039 GERMANY DEP 9 Wimpern Geschutz (stamp)	Socket head. Ca. 1890. Hair eyelashes. Open mouth. 20" D - E

SH 1040 15 DEP	Shoulder head. Open mouth. Ca. 1899. 25″ E - F
SH 1059 DEP 2	Socket head (swivel) on shoulder plate. Upper torso wood covered with kid. Fashion body. Open mouth. 19″ E - F
SH 1075	Socket head. Open mouth. 17″ D - E
1078 GERMANY SIMON & HALBIG S & H 3	Socket head. Open mouth. Ca. 1905. 32″ F - G
HALBIG HANDWERCK 1079 DEP GERMANY 13½	Made for Heinrich Handwerck. 1895. Open mouth. Socket head. 37″ F - H
S & H 1079 DEP	Socket head. Open mouth. 1896. 12″ A - B
S H 1080 DEP 9	Shoulder head. Open mouth. 22″ D - E
SH 1081	Shoulder head. Closed mouth. 22″ $325.00
S & H 1099	Oriental. Olive socket head. Open mouth. 14″ L - M
GERMANY 1129 SIMON & HALBIG S & H	Olive socket head. Open mouth. 13″ L - M
1159 GERMANY SIMON & HALBIG S & H 7	Socket head. Adult body. Ca. 1905. 25″ J - K
S & H 1160 GERMANY 2	Shoulder head. Closed mouth. 10″ C - D
1170 SH 6½ D	Shoulder head. Open mouth. 14″ B - C
S & H 1199	Olive socket head. Open mouth. 15″ M - N

GERMANY
S & H
1242 DEP

Socket head. Open mouth. 16" C - D

1248
SIMON & HALBIG
S & H 5

Socket head. Open mouth. 16" C - D

S & H 1249 DEP
GERMANY SANTA

Made for Hamburger & Co. 1901. Socket head. Open mouth. 20" E - F

S H 1250
DEP GERMANY 4

Shoulder head. Open mouth. 24" E - F

S & H
1254
GERMANY

Shoulder head. Open mouth. 18" C - D

SH 1260 DEP
GERMANY 6

Shoulder head. Open mouth. 16" D - E

S & H 1279
GERMANY
2

Socket head. Open mouth. 24" D - E

S & H 1279 DEP
GERMANY 7½

Socket head. Open mouth. Musical mechanical doll. 18" H - I

SIMON & HALBIG
1280
DEP
GERMANY

Shoulder head. Open mouth. 16" D - E

SIMON & HALBIG
1290 A8
MADE IN GERMANY

Shoulder head. Open mouth. 16" D - E

1294
SIMON & HALBIG
MADE IN GERMANY
40

Socket head. Open mouth. 24" E - F